BUS.

Please renew or return items by the date
shown on your receipt

www.hertsdirect.org/libraries

Renewals and
enquiries: 0300 123 4049

Textphone for hearing   0300 123 4041
or speech impaired

Hertfordshire

D1334323

H46 507 445 4

The Frost Fairs

by

JOHN MCCULLOUGH

SALT

LONDON

PUBLISHED BY SALT PUBLISHING
Acre House, 11–15 William Road, London NW1 3ER, United Kingdom

© John McCullough, 2010

The right of John McCullough to be identified as the
author of this work has been asserted by him in accordance
with Section 77 of the Copyright, Designs and Patents Act 1988.

Salt Publishing 2010
Reprinted with corrections 2011

Printed and bound in the United Kingdom by CPI Antony Rowe

Typeset in Swift 9.5 / 13

ISBN 978 1 84471 398 1 paperback

Salt Publishing Ltd gratefully acknowledges
the financial assistance of Arts Council England

1 3 5 7 9 8 6 4 2

to Morgan Case, with all my love

Contents

Acknowledgements

I wish to thank the editors of the following publications in which some of these poems previously appeared: *Chroma, Cimarron Review, E-Verse, Fleeting, The Guardian, Magma, Poetry International, Poetry London, Reactions, Rhythm, The Rialto, Smiths Knoll, The Wolf*. 'Known Light' won First Prize in the Robin Lee memorial poetry competition, 2002 and 'The Other Side of Winter' won Second Prize in the *Chroma* international writing competition, 2008. Poems here have also featured in the pamphlets *Unplugged at Café Atlantic* (Waterloo, 2004), *Cloudfish* (Pighog, 2007) and *The Lives of Ghosts* (Tall-Lighthouse, 2008).

I'm also indebted to Tom Sargant for his help with Polari; Kate Summerscale whose biography of Marion "Joe" Carstairs, *The Queen of Whale Cay* inspired 'The Empress of Mud'; Antony Woodward and Robert Penn for compiling *The Wrong Kind of Snow*; K. M. Elisabeth Murray for *Caught in the Web of Words*, a biography of her dictionary-editing grandfather; Byron Rogers for his interview with the hangman Syd Dernley in *An Audience with an Elephant*; Quentin Crisp, whose remark on 'The horrors of peace' in *The Naked Civil Servant* is paraphrased in 'Georgie, Belladonna, Sid'; and Bob whose cabbie's blog Taxi Tales (www.taxistorys.blogspot.com) spurred the writing of 'The Long Mile'. I wish to thank everyone who has commented on the poems here in various forms in writing groups or individually, including Julia Bird, David Briggs, Robert Hamberger, Maria Jastrzebska, Gareth Jones, Helen Mort, Helen Oswald, Janet Sutherland, Ben Wilkinson and Jackie Wills. Special thanks go to Alfred Corn, Roddy Lumsden and Catherine Smith for their kindness and wise words.

Sleeping Hermaphrodite

Asleep? I'm watching you through my lids.
This isn't easy, tracking your nebulous shape
while you assess my neck's turn, slide
down to smooth cleavage, tummy, waist

then encounter what's stashed below my thigh.
Here I am, unveiled as arguable,
a mishmash of harbour and ship—the stay
in thought when all ideas are possible.

I'm everything yet deeply ill-equipped
for solitude. What I need to know
is whether you ache to prise free

the ankle I've left loosely wrapped
in a sheet. Singlespeak is boring. Let's talk toes
and honey. Come on, nosey boy. Surprise me.

Talacre

where we turned off the dissolving path
to chance uncertain territory. High dunes

like hills of sugar, so smooth we lost whole feet
but found ourselves again, defied dense sky

by making our own light. We followed
the roaming fence and, like the rabbits

darting over marram, were never caught out.
We reached a new country, the sea

at first too far and blocked by swerving
channels—mercury in the dimness—

but we weren't afraid to innovate,
rolling up trousers for running jumps,

splatting down with a squelch to write names
in sand among the casualties

of starfish, bladderwrack. Messy letters,
our fingers digging past the first resistance,

our only witnesses the wind turbines way out—
a sleepy, inaudible crowd, two so close

to each other from our perspective, we swore
they must have occupied the same dream.

Night Writing

In humid months, at the estate's unwatched edge,
the boys gather for an after-hours cigarette

before trashing field gates. All boast Reeboks, earrings,
their honed geezer-laughs rev-revving

with the engines of graffiti-tagged bangers.
Customized stereos thump out speed garage,

the race kicking off in a blizzard of chalk dust,
their bouncing charge towards a crooked iron post.

Death and dew ponds can't stop them while they swerve
past quivering teasel, conquer the bone ridge's turn,

skeins of wool lifting from gorse as banners
for the night's whooping, fist-raising winners.

Further off, the crews unite for a slow drift, melt into hills
but leave the empty sky with headlamp trails:

blazing ghosts still performing their necessary work,
still scribbling their names on the dark.

Reading Frank O'Hara on the Brighton Express

I might believe we are stationary.
It's only everything out there kindly
hurtling past, the grey verticals of Clapham
revealed as bars of a song. I might lend my ear
to catch cirrus chit-chat then touch down
at Gatwick and watch parked cars nuzzle
in tidy rows. Which reminds me to sort
my manners out, to raise a hand to waving trees
whizzing backwards, plastic bags in their branches
brilliant flags announcing carnivals
in Balcombe, Wivelsfield, Hassocks.

I could trill like a starling myself, bless everything
outside and within this case of human fireworks:
the silver-chained lads probing Burger King bags
like lucky dips; the Tannoy woman who is Our Lady,
surely, with a mobile altar of Ribena and Coke;
the suits with *Guardian*s hiding *Heat* magazine.

I could twig that Brighton is unreal,
is being made as we approach,
the shops plugged in, the prom laid down,
the new beach scattered with smiling pebbles,
there where buses have names
so we can get knocked down by Dusty Springfield.

I might conjure up crowds auditioning
for the North Laine, all dreadlocks and posturing,
benefits and big schemes, with different kinds
of queen walking different kinds of dog—
vital clutter that dashes or repairs
Brighton dreams, that brings death or a boon
for the West Pier, swaying over the surf.

It all glides on towards salt-caked houses
and the united panes of Betjeman's station,
though it's not him but you, Frank, who I picture
in the station café, coughing your lungs out
above a latte as you eye the black waiter.

In just a moment I shall pass the gates
of heaven and find you,
my memories of travel left in the ticket machine
as we stroll out down Queens Road,
the sun on our skin, the sea shining so whitely
that we stop and stare, and keep on staring.

The Light of Venus

October evenings see this avenue climb
to space. Lit rooms hover in the icy dark.
I gaze from my kitchen like an astronaut

at street lamp stars, the buckthorn stretching
for the light of Venus. *No two planets,*
you said, *come closer than Earth and her,*

the smaller world swinging towards us as she spins
wrongly, remembering an ancient impact,
proposing union then veering out of range.

I stroke the edge of my laptop,
consider your email's transatlantic journey.
A blackbird skitters across maple leaves,

canary yellow shirts, their summer
hoards of sugars transmuted to carotene.
I remember the cruel heat of August

when our dripping bodies flew
to shelter in the park as thunder started.
Beneath a whitebeam, our fingers locked.

Now everything retreats to its sap.
Even the wind wants a home to dive into.
On the net, a Venus probe reveals lightning

beneath clouds of acid. Is the planet closer still,
now we know this secret? And on that world
where a day is longer than a year,

is it really lightning with no trees to run for,
no creatures to race towards sanctuary
then clutch each other, retrieving their breath?

Masterclass

He never tired of explaining from his stool
the route to an immaculate Guinness.

Tilt your glass at forty-five degrees
to kill the splash. Hold it close

to the spout, avoiding contact. Take the brew
three-quarters up, then leave to settle.

What's done next is the barman's choice.
I liked to guess who he'd escort to the gents —

the young drag queen? The bear?
Toot like chalk on the black lid,

his eyes impish as he crept back to his squeeze
for hugs or squabbles. I'd get yanked in

to arbitrate, to remember whens and hows
while I tipped piled fag butts into bins.

The last time he left abruptly, before I could try
my fancy Shamrock, the stale heat relieved

by a blast of salty air. He never worked out
who he caught the virus from

and he didn't end his final class
with the ideal ratio of white to black.

Twelve years on, I haven't stopped waiting
to finish pouring that pint.

Small, Vertical Pleasures

They are trialling pills for weightless environments
where bones are partly metabolized,
the heart switches to limping pace.

The task: to go to bed and stay a year.
Three hundred and seventy days lying
by a NO SITTING sign, ten to a room.

My fingers ache to stretch for lost pencils.
I have given up learning Macedonian,
explore instead the ceiling's furtive map.

I know the name of each country there,
discover in quirks of plaster a wealth
of dark histories, the festering of ideals.

Down here, geometry reigns. D smiles at me
from a cruel angle. I tire of P more each day:
his shrunken ear, stoicism, loud masturbation.

They move disputants, rearrange us
like dominoes. Squashing cartons is a treat.
I tear mine into jigsaws, effigies of women.

I understand we shall need two months
to readjust to gravity's embrace, to learn again
standing up, how to walk, how to fall.

K, who left with threats of violence last week,
will not receive his cheque but is a better man.
I wish him a swift return to tea with no straw,

a path following the upright lines of joy.
I want him to lie in a city park, gazing
at poplars and skyscrapers, then rise

and take his place among them.

On Galileo's Birthday

I asked and, whoops, you bought a universe
from B&Q. A bowl of cacti, each one a fat galaxy
of spiny stars. Or are they more specific zodiacs?
Unyielding trio, do they steer our lives like Fates?
I can't remember life without them, feel if we sifted
their hemisphere of soil and broken bricks we'd find
only a puzzle of abstract roots, no graspable trace
of what keeps us awake on cold moonless nights,
plotting outer and earthly and inner space.

Sneakers

They invaded Pacific shallows without a sound,
the reply to a beachcomber's prayer.
Tabloid gold, the storm which jounced their ship,
El Niño that ordered Alaska to *Just Do It*.
Their saviours, air-cushioned soles:
unexpected life jackets that pump us with hope
though it's the missing I can't forget,
those resolute types that rode foam for weeks,
questing under Sirius and a fairy-tale moon
to reach palm leaves, a slow, glorious fade.

Known Light

Now you're crossing that ocean, I have to confess
I've rather warmed to this shed where nothing is yours,
where your father consulted a sacred Bunsen flame.

Chipped oak, a gas tap, scores of powdered specimens—
the perfect stage for resurrecting my 'A' Level Chemistry.
I remember this much: each metal has a secret,

unchangeable colour. A Nichrome wire dipped
in compounds, then in fire, bares their truer shades.
It's a bit like those stars, the ones you rehearsed

on the pebbles at Kemp Town: the blood
in Betelgeuse, Rigel's constant blue—they show
only with a telescope's fiercer attention.

You have to inspire electrons if you want to unveil
calcium's brick red, barium's green,
the strange lilac which simply means *potassium*.

Loyal friends, they return now with the tiniest prod,
make me smug as an alchemist,
impatient for knowledge of the lone unlabelled jar.

Reveal yourself, sweet familiar, I whisper to glass
before I'm blinded by the white heat
of a magnesium heart.

The Last Hangman

He sat beside me with his smile and slippers:
a lean man enthralled by my digital recorder,

his breezy wife interrupting with scones.
I stared at light fittings, keys on their hook.

He downed his tea, asked if I'd travelled far,
then flourished a noose from his tin.

It's all maths really — nothing tricky.
Tell me your weight and I'll work out your drop.

He was a wire that would not snap,
another England calmly holding out,

unfazed by a crowd of flapping shadows
from washing pegged over the lawn.

I left with a dry throat and crumbs on my sleeve,
the executioner grinning as my taxi set off

and he grew smaller, vanished beneath the road,
waving constantly, returning my gaze.

The Long Mile

Hello, I'm your driver tonight. I just guessed
from the shifts in the air you drink gin
and smoke weed, own a sax and a tongue
that might beg me to knock off a fiver.
Don't bother. And let me request at the start
no yelling *turn left* while you're pointing hard right
or *slow down* so the meter will plunge
into sleep. A snail's mile is a mile
and I'm honest and civil until
your pissed shag starts a fight with a seat.

∾

Unnerve me. It's hard but you'll get my respect.
Last year I pulled up at a house clean-detached
from reality. Spidering out came a nut
with a box and a book into which
he set down my replies to enquiries
on superstrings, God and the seven roads.
Angling inside, he flipped open the case of a bust
in grey stone with no shoulders. A cryptic expression—
half horror, half wonder. The lid snapped shut.
Now drive on but don't forget the head.

∾

The cursed gift of a listening face...
Sad stories unfurl in advance of top gear:
love conundrums in Cantonese, Spanish, Sumerian—
subtexts in ultrasound. Nod, glance, exhale.
The wild German girl yesterday died

three times for *lust* or for *Lars* or her *list*
though when dropped off appeared to feel better.
I met her again later on in a dream
as the voice of my sat-nav while crossing
the Gobi with Samuel Pepys. I was lost.

~

Sundays I catch up with fares from last night.
Casanovas, harassed by the glare of the sun,
leave strange flats with rough heads and fresh lies.
One claimed to have been a sloshed guest of the cells,
flapped the clear bag with his laces and lighter
but no charge sheet. Another laid bare
ECG scars from a faked heart attack—
though on seeing his shirts by the gate
in piled carriers, and the stereo balanced on top,
his white hand clutched his chest just the same.

~

Most of the time there aren't footnotes for guidance
on reading the masses' arrivals and flights.
They are library books for return the same hour.
Once, a comatose girl was slung
into the back with her baby and purse.
All the way, not a sound. Then no key
for the flat. What the hell do you do?
I deposited both by the door and made tracks
with my fare and a thousand bad dreams.
Never again will I take that dark backstreet.

~

The classic deceit sends me off on an endless
excursion to roads with no houses or punters.
You wish. The clone city inside my brain's maze
has door numbers, pear trees and little-known fountains,
its history written in scratches on railings.
Lost churches still glower as gaps in the skyline,
beneath it a covert and sacrosanct order.
My mind hunts out patterns untouched by bulldozers,
shapes that spring from and shuffle and clinch
one another like parts in a score. A ballad in tarmac.

~

Time to get out: the smashed moon's lost in cloud
and, though doubtless not quite where you thought,
the law says you pay. But before you rub coins
I would ask you to check there's no phone
or novelty socks on the seat to disturb
the head I'm about to invoke. The stone head
I still keep in the boot whose eyes say
We carry the ghosts of all travellers with us.
Sane or half-gone, cloud nine or listless,
there's one journey only. It's never short-distance.

Islands

are everywhere you said, and pointed out
a leather glove stuck fast on sea-glazed pebbles.
Hoary stock that thrives when it's left to blemish
the milk-white cliffs with mauve. A rebel cloud
that should, for safety's sake, have joined the flock
of cumuli that rushed beneath. But no,
your islands were free countries, remote
yet still, perhaps, in reach for those with pluck.

I was nestled in your bath that night, mulling over
a distant grove of shaving brushes
when I heard you snorting on the phone.
Love? I think I'll stick to lovers.
I turned the tap to drown your voice with splashes
and felt the water rise inside my boat.

The Floating World

At noon, the sunlight ricochets off white cliffs.
The oystercatcher blasts its *kleep-a-kleep*
but no one's listening. In ruptured chalk, fossils

of iguanodon and mammoth strive
for attention, claw over hoof. Flattened limbs
stretch wide, a tableau of thirst.

Their numbers grow. Two months ago
a cyclist racing by the undercliff wall
was slammed down, dragged out to sea.

It took three days for his remains to find the shore.
Oceanographers spoke of a hundred-mile journey
dictated by currents, particulars of shape:

some beaches collect right gloves,
others left. Either way, what is lost returns,
emptied but clutching the air.

I dreamed of his body that night, his slim hands
flat on the water, bleached face swathed
in channel wrack, eyes larvikite blue.

I had to phone you, an ocean away in New York.
But, though we'd talked the day before,
while it was ringing, ringing

you became dead too. I pictured you
suspended in rock, silent, reaching out
from a crowd of frozen men.

You picked up and I made you describe
all you could feel and hear and smell:
your jagged fingernail, a busker's horn, the box

of fetid plums left outside your flat
all week. As well as any voices could, we proved
your body's life then planned your journey back.

I spend my days till then skulking in the cliffs'
shadows, unearthing whelks' eggs, skeins
of dulse. And though you're safe, I know

those other floating men must find me.
Lying on chalk, I wait for them, arms outstretched,
where the rock pools meet the sea.

The Other Side of Winter

Overnight the Thames begins to move again.
The ice beneath the frost fair cracks. Tents,
merry-go-rounds and bookstalls glide about

on islands given up for lost. They race,
switch places, touch — the printing press nuzzling
the swings — then part, slip quietly under.

Still, there is no end of crystal weather.
I hoard coal, stare mostly at the chimney's back,
fingering the pipe he gave me on the quay.

Even now it carries his greatcoat's whiff:
ale, oranges, resolve. I remember his prison-ship
lurking out from shore, huge as Australia.

I'll write, my dear sweet man, he said,
then squeezed my thigh and turned, a sergeant
again, bellowing at a flock of convicts.

I do not have the nerve to light it.
The mouthpiece is covered with teeth marks, sweat.
I look out at my museum-garden,

the shrubs locked in glass cases,
the latticework a galaxy of frozen dew.
There is no snow in New South Wales.

I cannot put the pipe down. It makes things happen.
Last week I heard a crash and ran outside to find
a jackdaw flat on the lawn. It must have fallen

from the sky, its wings locked together
by hardened sleet, its neck twisted as though broken
from straining to see the incredible.

The Dictionary Man

Sometimes the quest seems hopeless; recently, for example,
the word art *utterly baffled me for several days*
— JAMES MURRAY, first editor of
the *Oxford English Dictionary*

I am inside the language, suspended
at my desk between *abject* and *abjure*.
My devils are the weight and texture of sounds,
the particular smile raised by my beloved's
use of *asinine*, the tang it leaves at the back
of the throat. I am doing this for English

but words are made of air. Quotations flap off
in draughts. The other day I found
alter ego under our bed. I have fifty
sorts of *abusion*, not even five of *abuse*.
There are too many expressions for how
I am feeling: imprinted, blurred at my edges.

D, *K* and *T* wait in pasteboard boxes
at the door, welcoming as Cerberus.
When opening *R*, I discovered a dead rat.
I have lost the eighteenth century and Mr Tyler
holds *Gr* to ransom, the *vawse/vaze*
debate stubbornly refusing to pass.

The ghost words enter my dreams.
They slide about my head on street signs,
messages from my love. *The almakoot*
is closing in. I am avunted, darling.
Please help. I wake at my desk, chastened
and sweating, encrusted with names.

Georgie, Belladonna, Sid

Paper, scissors, stone. Grinning poster boys
for Winston's bona home front, the flashing sky
pink as a boudoir. Sid's craggy martinis thump

away with a powder puff to the gramophone
trills of 'There's a Small Hotel'. My eek hovers
above Lady B's sink, bleach storming my scalp.

*Open your aunt nells, dear. No beauty
without agony.* Bitch. A zhooshy recruit,
I have plucked and plucked to prove devotion,

my fitness for trolling and jitterbugging
in prearranged gloom. Kohl, rouge, bronze lipstick.
Steadfast sisters, we tarry like Fates on the periphery

of guest-houses where forces are stationed,
B stitching sequins to maroon gloves by the light
of a tissue-papered torch. Sid bats his ogle riahs

in ten minute spells. We're the bang they want
to go out with, saintly omi-palones who fall
when we stroke the Polish navy's smooth serges.

Talk is ruthless: weather, duties, family—
bevvy at mine? My favourite's a Yank.
Ed Paxton, his fluent hands unknotting the rope

of my body, loosening dreams that have never been,
will never be freer. Between his legs
I'm the right shape, intrepid, all-seeing.

The horrors of peace are many. Street lamps slam on
beside snapping bunting, thrashed Union flags.
What's wrong with your eyebrows? my brother says.

I stare blankly back, incapable of irony,
laughter. Sid moves to Orkney — *Bless her
Chatsworth Road heart* — has five dolly feelies.

Belladonna signs up for the merchant navy.
She writes to me, praising *bijou striped curtains,
black sailors, the Atlantic's sharp smell*

though I do not reply. I linger here, still paper
but folding, folding. The streets swarm with mammoth
skirts, decency, bedsits. I've used the last smudge

of American shampoo. Each dusk I vada
the ripped-open, scattered rose sky and pray
to God for the safe return of my blackout.

Glossary of Polari Words

Polari is the English homosexual and theatrical slang prevalent in the early to mid 20th century.

bona — lovely; *martinis* — hands; *eek* — face; *aunt nells* — ears; *zhooshy* — tarted up; *trolling* — mincing; *ogle riahs* — eyelashes; *omi-palones* — effeminate men; *bevvy* — drink; *dolly* — beautiful; *feelies* — children; *bijou* — small; *vada* — look at

Angels Over Hatfield

We wake to rattling, a warped ceiling,
the small house being slapped like a drum.

Part of outside wants in, though Christ knows
what would hunger for bottle-green carpet

and box bedrooms thrown up after the war.
Then a sucking noise, a squall of dust

and the cheap, shallow-pitched roof
peels away into night, trailing wires as kite tails.

We're blown utterly open, an old moon
scrutinizing stained trousers and sheets.

A flash from next door: their roof's climbing too
then a third, twenty more—aluminium angels

thrusting into the troposphere, pulling
the street with them as they gather and wheel.

No one has told them they cannot soar,
that a roof's life is to sit like a lid.

Beyond pylons and beeches, they clank
as they vibrate on gales, testing their nerve.

Why should they care for futures
while they curve through each moment so fiercely,

young beasts charging through starlight,
colliding like cymbals inside the clouds?

The Empress of Mud

Christmas: dust clouds and sand flies.
The natives and I are laying a road across
my island. I demonstrate each step: an empress
crouching to bash rock with a tiny mallet,
like this. Nods all round, sundry errors.
The clearing tractor veers slowly off course.

Lonely? I have too many friends to waste time
staring at women's necks, to write letters
to a moon-faced girl in London, explaining
why I cannot return. There are flamingos
in my garden. I am in Wonderland.
Perhaps I shall put down a lawn for croquet.

On every side, the gluey tongues
of hibiscus. Foolish hummingbirds disappear
down boas' throats. My project will not finish.
An empire must forever be improvised,
imagined—coffee made with brackish water
from the wells, crab fed to the chickens.

They lay fishy eggs. Everything in my domain
smells of fish. I do not mind. I hang
barracuda from lime trees, watch them swing.
The man-woman, they say. She who rules
from her palace of bottles and mud
where, when it rains, it rains in every room.

I cannot sleep. I rise in darkness then drift
towards the mangrove's unsolvable tangles
and a sea cow that reveals herself
as a mermaid. Each night she swims
from England, demanding answers.
And nothing I say or build is good enough.

The Crystal Palace

In Hyde Park, leeches are waiting.
Their glass prisons are linked
to a bell by fine chains. It rings

when they become frenzied by shifts
in the air that signify unfurling tempests.
You would have relished such enterprise,

this Exhibition dreamt up by the Prince—
halls of crystal where any world is feasible.
I picture your long fingers caressing

the rims of improbable fountains,
grasping mangos from Assam, the sides
of a bed that turns into a life-raft.

But you are oceans away, a sunburnt jailer
flanked by swamps and blood-sucking convicts.
And I am an envelope-making machine.

I slide through grinning crowds for sights
to furnish next week's letter, mark the days
between replies. *A knife with eighty blades*,

I shall write, *might be practical for pioneers.*
What arms the colonist like imagination?
By a wall are models of the human eye

cross-sectioned, a doctor pointing
to cornea, pupil, nerve to demonstrate
how light can flood a structure, then leave.

Circumference

In Alexandria, on the longest day
the chief librarian bent down
beside a sundial to measure the world.

He linked its pillar's height and shadow
to an angle in Syene where at solstice
the sun glares straight down a well.

From this: a magic sum, a number
men can carry which encircles
the earth, reveals the size of everything.

Me, I have my doubts about the fervour
he has caused, these hordes who press
for news about the next, more vast expanse.

The sky isn't tall enough. Stars
will never do. There was talk last month
of plotting the distance to the afterlife.

The librarian proclaimed the age
of final answers. I hear tonight a priestess
plans to ring his house with dung.

Miss Fothergill Observes a Snail

Of course, it could be a hallucination,
this drowsy afternoon under the chestnut.
Robert's topiary knight is a fraction too vivid,
the snail ascending my chair leg oversized,
overexposed. A spaniel bullets across the Sussex lawn.
I sip tonic as Lord Wakefield sternly peels his orange,
an English summer dismantling around him.

No plovers' eggs at lunch — a giant wave
of dollar signs has breached the chalk cliffs.
He hawks Queen Anne tables, nails down a smile.
I too have retreated: a frigid companion
weighed up by maids at windows.
A Cubist parody, all angles as I break
in my heels, this freshly-waxed skin.

When alone, I am fidgety, distrustful:
a soldier still, delirious in the Cambrai sun.
My firstborn self whispers against me, pokes through
each deep vowel. Always the impulse
to sprawl and stuff pockets, to build again
a gentleman's reputation — here a cigar,
there a nickname, a passion for squash and fair play.

I adjust my buff cotton skirt, the pleats
above my organ that in puberty divided
meetings of the Sexological Society. On advice
I restrict myself to flirtation and friendship.
It is a question of pragmatism, of dressing
the wound. The snail, frustrated by the chair's rim,
takes an upside-down journey underneath.

My treasured Lord meanwhile hacks
at stubborn pith with his penknife, a schoolboy
scattering rind and juice. I take the blade
and slip it under the last island of peel.
He blushes and smiles, different now,
palpable. I notice for the first time
small, delicate hairs on his ear.

The spaniel lumbers into the shade,
tongue dangling, and flops. It's too bright out there.
There is more than company in the shadows.
The air goes quiet and still enough to identify,
far away, the insistence of the sea. And I feel it
in my belly, at the ends of my fingers:
a rising force, the next inescapable birth.

Foucault's Spoons

Genet, Barthes, Julie Christie: we've kissed them all
but our master's thick lips are still our favourites.

His slow steps create pandemonium in the drawer—
a high-pitched ring that could splinter a goblet—

till we're dumbstruck when he yanks us back
into the light. Inevitably, he's prepared himself

something astounding, his arguments
for aniseed or lime sanctified by his tongue.

Lying there, we can taste stranger residues:
hash, the tang of semen. It's a spoon's version of heaven;

he'll never guess, but we sigh the whole time
as we meet the abrasions of scourer and cloth,

as he nests us precisely on top of each other
and the dark swallows us.

Cold Fusion

March thaws the ocean
and I resume spinning pebbles into the shoal.
Speedboats reclaim the lavender distance,
their backwash diminished
by rollers that hiss at my feet.

On jetties, men clank huge buckets of mussels,
their rubber soles squelching
past crate stacks, flung rope.
The air stinks of spilt fish guts and tainted jokes.
Husband comes home to find his wife . . .

Last month, they hoisted a dead man
from the glass-covered Atlantic,
a small crowd of us watching.
Matted blond hair, his face purple and mustard.
He seemed to be pondering inscrutable algebra.

A passing nurse crossed herself,
two boys dashed for a bus and I carried on home,
trying to remember your smell.
It's my turn to phone your mother
though I'll write a letter instead:

calm words that say everything's fine.
In my recurring dream, I swim
instinctively back to Christmas
to sweep again all the icicles
from under your bedroom window.

Ghost

I couldn't see them, but your smoking wicks
seemed proof enough that wraiths were hanging round.
Seduced like me by clutter, they frowned
at you beside heaped film reels, stacks of books.

Night after night in a director's chair
you shut your eyes and gathered up the masses:
slender women at war with enormous dresses.
Move the candle flame to show you're there.

In dreams, I'd ask if you were a hallucination,
you who stroked my chipped glass bangle
instead of the wrist inside, who fiercely gripped
the copper headboard but refused all ministrations.
I returned one day to a silent room lit by a candle.
Sliding through shadows, I blew it out and stopped.

The Cure

Then, once your plan's been thwarted, seek relief
where fulmars rasp and dive from sudden cliffs.

Stand there, knee-deep in swash, to know
the glide of spume from lunging hills, to view

the rock pools' effortless birth,
white stones emerging like first teeth.

Sun arrows off chalk — below, behind
and through you, all answers close at hand,

the surf explaining. Relax and you'll clarify
to air, the seascape branded on each eye.

Take the scars. Cherish them. Stagger home.
And when you're feeling mended, pass this on.

Portrait of the Young Poet as a Wagtail

He prefers a life of battlements, a ledge
close to collapse and astounding gusts of spray.
Looking up, he meets a crag's flint-eyed gaze
with his own black stare then rests,
contained. A good night is spent losing
himself in history, the chalk's tales
of when it roamed in brine. He studies waves
in darkness and discovers music

not in the smash of breakers—the stock
din of a well-drilled battalion's charge—
but the clatter of billows hauled back
through pebbles, the trickles that finger
what's already clean and murmur
only of cliff falls, the separated stars.

The Moon of Myths

rides low tonight,
a face fingered by poplars,
locked in glasses of water,
jazz musicians' dreams.

To Greek soldiers this was Selene:
the haloed flirt who smirked
just yards beyond lobbed spears
or the wings of Icarus.

I prefer more humble views—
these lampposts' stoic glow
as if the larger light
might gather their spilt change.

Slim, unfeathered pagans
with a quieter faith—
they are waiting for white streets
that are old, untravelled.

Severance

It niggled you, that wooden chair
tossed in brambles by other residents.
Its long, white bones, deformed
by winter, kept urging you to buttress
an arm scratched well beyond repair.
You propped it up in sunlight to document
its rust and meagre paint, performed
with your Kodak a split-second kindness

then grabbed it from behind, an expert mugger;
held a stern Doc Marten on its back
and jerked and slammed till stiff legs severed.
I felt each strident, drawn-out crack
then met your eyes as you delivered
your *all done* smile, a low, contented chuckle.

Seascape

Scaling hills, we clump through heavy air.
A missing sun's tarnished light
tints the Downs with lovat, smoke.

But coastal turf gives a bounce
to our feet. You have returned to me
as surely as a season and we're defined

by what's glimpsed yet fully present:
skylarks that shoot their liquid songs
from fescue; an adder unwrapping itself

in shade; staunch houndstongue and rampion,
flouting their odds. Each step takes me
further into the seascape of you:

your shifting weather, firm bedrock,
shore carved by old lovers, a stream
that hesitates then charges into shoal.

Squeezing your hand, I consider glasswort,
its wait in salt marsh for an engulfing wave.
I think of a man who's stared for hours

at a chalk cliff, digesting its barrenness,
who sees a flint vibrate its wings
and spiral away into sky.

The Disappearance of St Anthony's Church

Hard to tell exactly when it vanished—
local rumour says late or early summer.
They stole the thing discreetly, brick by brick,
an anti-miracle. Curt officials blame
the village but no infidel's been punished,
the two best clues a chisel by a tomb,
a distant maze of tyre marks from a truck—
though some insist that these came later.

They left behind foundations, one unwanted wall
and a different view of pines, the snaking river.
Next spring the first grass sprouted in the nave,
the chancel's earth disturbed only by lovers
and the odd partridge hunting for snails
or a place to rest in silence for a while.

Tropospheric

Clouds know one word and always sing it.
Roughly translated it is *change*
though with inflection it can mean
grow, *unite* or *decay*. Icebergs puzzle clouds
because they are locked stiff
and cannot join in with air anthems
or life itself, which is a wind rolling
through a cloud, shaping its change.

Cloud sex—or merging and changing—
complicates matters because it makes
it hard to remember who they are
or were. This is why clouds sound a low note
after birds plunge through them:
for that one moment they are distinct.

The alien firmness of those that share
the skyways leads tragic-minded clouds
to believe heaven is far below
and they are in changing hell.
After rain the air is full of such sad ones
left behind to mourn the departed
above lakes, rivers and oceans.

Rumour has it one day these dead will return
en masse and the sea will be completely
in the sky for ever, bringing the end
of change as clouds know it—
no more sex and no more songs,
just one big cloud
and one enormous, impossible word.

Dragons

Empty carriages fill our afternoon,
your breath smoky from winter as you slide

through each door. Your left arm, tattooed,
sports a red dragon that has lightened

to the pink of your lip. Your grin opens
as bare fingers discover my zip.

The Amazing Tintin

sucks ice cubes at a bar, gazes out to sea.
Tintin without Haddock who he left

with a question mark hanging beside his beard.
Tintin in his blue sweater, who wants to help

glum skinheads but gets asked to the sauna.
Snowy's run away. The boy's forgotten

how Calculus wandered off. He's growing
stubble and his wet hair won't lift

for the next frame. Where are
the frames anyway? Where, when people collide,

are the coloured stars, the ragged
RRRING of the telephone?

He spits ice in the glass. He can smell
adventures out there: smugglers doubling

as drag queens, treasure under the old pier
but he's stopped too long. He's lost

the maps and tonight for one last time Haddock,
cranky, devoted Haddock, will drink

himself to sleep aboard his ship.

for Cathy Martin

Between Beak and Pincer

He started with squids:
two columns of tentacles etched
over his biceps, his eyes tracking the needle.

Then images came flickering
like half-recalled films: slapstick otters
or thrush assassins, blue veins as swung worms,

each shape snuggling
into a human-sized jigsaw,
a zoo of ink he preferred to call *my cocoon*.

Still they kept swarming:
unreadable marks which could form
a pincer or one more beak, jungles inside tigers.

Removals would scar him;
he couldn't sink frogs with skin grafts,
watch his adder's diamonds lasered off, scale by scale.

And who was better dressed
for seduction when no stranger could shun
that monkey puzzle of tails, those many secret mouths?

Cherry Tops

It's a problem all right, the logistics
of masking your beard shadow in a jerking
patrol car when you've only one eye.
Especially when you're half-cut.
Especially when you need air but the rear
windows are locked and there's no word
from beyond the suspect transport enclosure.
I trick the lid off my compact and attack
my chin, the bulk at least smothered
before the mirror's lost in a dust storm
of Dual Perfection Mahogany.

It's not my fault but hers, the woman
I'm trying to coax back. St Chi-Chi amplifies
everything, reckons *It's my Divine right.*
One snide glance from The Baboon
and it was cabaret time — profanities flying
with the Sambucas before she flipped
my cerebral cortex to CHARGE
and the three of us plunged
downstairs. The full *Dynasty* tumble,
my right eye and half my water-balloon
cleavage left squashed on the banister
as she vanished with the light.

Cherry tops, they called police cars
in sixties Hollywood. It made them sound
so wonderfully feminine. I extend
a leg from the fluorescent, yellow-checked
Astra and try my best to breathe
slowly, to focus on my quest

for a proper mirror and loo roll to refill
my basque so there's a trace of her
for the interview. An air of proportion.
No lipstick on her teeth as she pleads
provocation, fingers crossed,
white nails providentially unbroken.

The Loft Fire

I used to wish I'd been there.
Not to rescue the Mac,
not to sigh in any undue
affection for shelves
but to climb into the room slowly,
the way I scaled an oak as a boy:
eyes on handholds till I entered
a chlorophyll sky,
joining spiders and insects
I never saw, just sensed waiting.

But when I stood at the foot
of the ladder weeks later
I couldn't think a green thought,
couldn't imagine fire or smoke,
only this: a blanket of leaves,
brittle and cold; a torrent of moths
swirling down through the hatch
till I was wearing a brown suit;
their paper wings folding—
a thousand closing doors.

Crepuscular

It's the hour everything
on the street squeezes into itself,
when walls or a ladder
are on the cusp
before waves sweep in
or the new regime starts—
the one with the trees in charge.

Sun is thrown on a wet road
and you find yourself nodding,
feel your barren mouth opening
for coins of light,
the lampposts' orange moons
bursting Clio bonnets.

Leaves are smaller gods now.
And the woman opposite,
leaning over a cup,
will someday come to own
all she might crave.

Except, of course, the field mouse,
the one from her dream,
its eager head twisting
through the hedge like *yes*.

Motile

What sticks is the hum
of the fridge in your basement,
a plane ticket lying flat on one chair.
The way, fag in hand, you order me to stop smoking:
you'll damage your cilia

and you conjure those tiny threads stroking together,
pushing wayward particles where they belong.
You drain a glass of vodka,
write my name in your diary beneath the date
when you'll wake in a new country.

You keep your promise:
two hours and twenty dollars on a dodgy line
from a city without Marmite
where you tussle with silverfish
and baseball shirt slang.

O much assailed friend,
in these fathomless times
I walk down to the ocean at night
to set my hand on its skin
and my mind on rowing, rowing, rowing.